MW00711030

Essentials of Co-operative Education.

George Jacob Holyoake

Essentials of Co-operative Education.
Holyoake, George Jacob
British Library, Historical Print Editions
British Library
1898].
19 p. ; 8°.
12273.k.9.(6.)

The BiblioLife Network

This project was made possible in part by the BiblioLife Network (BLN), a project aimed at addressing some of the huge challenges facing book preservationists around the world. The BLN includes libraries, library networks, archives, subject matter experts, online communities and library service providers. We believe every book ever published should be available as a high-quality print reproduction; printed on- demand anywhere in the world. This insures the ongoing accessibility of the content and helps generate sustainable revenue for the libraries and organizations that work to preserve these important materials.

The following book is in the "public domain" and represents an authentic reproduction of the text as printed by the original publisher. While we have attempted to accurately maintain the integrity of the original work, there are sometimes problems with the original book or micro-film from which the books were digitized. This can result in minor errors in reproduction. Possible imperfections include missing and blurred pages, poor pictures, markings and other reproduction issues beyond our control. Because this work is culturally important, we have made it available as part of our commitment to protecting, preserving, and promoting the world's literature.

GUIDE TO FOLD-OUTS, MAPS and OVERSIZED IMAGES

In an online database, page images do not need to conform to the size restrictions found in a printed book. When converting these images back into a printed bound book, the page sizes are standardized in ways that maintain the detail of the original. For large images, such as fold-out maps, the original page image is split into two or more pages.

Guidelines used to determine the split of oversize pages:

• Some images are split vertically; large images require vertical and horizontal splits.
• For horizontal splits, the content is split left to right.
• For vertical splits, the content is split from top to bottom.
• For both vertical and horizontal splits, the image is processed from top left to bottom right.

❧ ESSENTIALS ❧

– OF –

CO-OPERATIVE

.. EDUCATION,

BY

GEORGE JACOB HOLYOAKE.

THE LABOUR ASSOCIATION

FOR

Promoting Co-operative Production based on the Co-partnership
of the Workers.

Central Office:

15, SOUTHAMPTON ROW, HOLBORN, LONDON, W.C.

[FOURPENCE

LABOUR ASSOCIATION

— FOR —

Promoting Co-operative Production based on Co-partnership of the Workers.

Central Office—15, SOUTHAMPTON ROW, HOLBORN, LONDON, W.C.
ESTABLISHED 1883.

President:	Hon. Legal Adviser:
F. MADDISON, M P	J. M. LUDLOW, C.B.

Hon. Treasurer:
ANEURIN WILLIAMS.

Vice-Presidents:

THE DUKE OF WESTMINSTER.
EARL GREY.
THE EARL OF STAMFORD.
LORD WANTAGE.
BISHOP OF DURHAM.
BISHOP OF RIPON.
HON. T. A. BRASSEY.
F. A. CHANNING, M.P.
HON. DADABHAI NAOROJI
FRANK BALLARD.

THOMAS BLANDFORD.
WILLIAM CAMPBELL.
HODGSON PRATT.
A. K. CONNELL.
E. O. GREENING.
JOSEPH GREENWOOD.
G. J. HOLYOAKE.
Miss H. MADDEN.
Professor MARSHALL.

Editor of "Labour Co-partnership":
Miss S. GURNEY.

Secretary:
HENRY VIVIAN.

WE earnestly ask the reader's attention to the important work which is being done by the Labour Association.

The work we set ourselves to do is not so much to raise our working people, as to help them to raise themselves. We think this is more effectual than alms-giving, and as hopeful as any movement of our time.

To advance the objects of the Association, the Committee desire the assistance of friends—(1) By helping to organise Meetings, Lectures, Conferences, Distribution of Literature amongst the Societies, Trade Unions, or Associations with which they may be connected; (2) By supplying the Committee with any information concerning the starting or position of any Co-operative Productive Societies in their district; (3) By becoming subscribers to the Association's funds of any sum not less than One Shilling per annum.

We respectfully invite all friends of social progress to become subscribers to the Association, and to assist in the extension of its work.

THE EXECUTIVE.

GEORGE JACOB HOLYOAKE.

ESSENTIALS

— OF —

CO-OPERATIVE ❋ EDUCATION,

BY

GEORGE JACOB HOLYOAKE.

•••••••••••••••••••

I.

[In one of the plays of Beaumont and Fletcher, a man is regarded as a traitor, who would confine kings to affairs "practical and honest." Happily in these days no such risk is incurred in counselling a movement, to lay deep the foundations of right purposes. The Labour Association, in common with other divisions of the Co-operative party, take interest in education. As I had often said that the ordinary conception of co-operative education did not include what those of us, who belonged to the earlier days of the movement, regarded as "essential," I was asked to make that plain. My answer was these addresses given in the Labour Association Rooms, Southampton Row, Holborn, June 22nd and July 6th, 1898; F. Maddison, M.P., in the chair.]

A PASSAGE by John Arthur Roebuck which meant much, as any passage of his did, explains my general object. His words were these: "Take the uneducated masses separately and talk to them. What do you find? Profound ignorance—inveterate prejudice. How then can the compound mass differ from the compound ingredients? There is no chemical fusion to make a hundred ignorant individuals one instructed mass."

There are no means of creating an "instructed mass" of co-operators save by the personal instruction of each.

Industrial co-operation implies the creation of a new sense. It means that in the pursuit of personal advantage, regard shall be had for the good of others. This is the very opposite of the Ishmael spirit of competition, which regards individual interests only. To care for the welfare of others is the first manifestation of the co-operative spirit. It alone brings fraternity into industry. Co-operation seeks to create and establish affection in labour and commerce, in the sense in which the great Lord Shaftesbury, of another century, was said to have a "private affection for public affairs." The affection I mean is not only for the collective triumphs of labour, but for the welfare of the worker.

Political economy teaches valuable lessons, but not this. It teaches how to acquire wealth, but nothing as to the duty of according an equitable share to all concerned in creating it. A distinct kind of education is needed for this. To make this clear, it is necessary to ask some questions.

For what does anyone want to join a co-operative society? Is it for dividend only? Is it for his own improvement, or both? Is it to promote the interest of others as well as his own? Is it to raise *as a class* those with whom he desires to associate? Does he know what the principles of the society are? Does he understand them if he does know them? Has he thought of their nature, their influence, and operation? What an advantage it would be to those who direct the affairs of a society, if every member had right knowledge of these things, into which no education scheme proposes to teach him. How much better it would be for the members if the questions, here recited, were asked of him. There would be co-operative education in them.

We are all acquainted with the member who is quite indifferent to the progress of the society to which he belongs—who never asks himself how far it is his duty, and how far it is in his power, to contribute to its prosperity. Will a knowledge of shorthand put this into his mind?

Eventually the apathetic member leaves the society altogether. What is the cause of that? What did he look forward to when he joined it? Was he ever instructed what to expect? It was written on the tombstone of one who died very young, "If I were so soon to be done for, I wonder what I was begun for." How many members have we whose co-operative education never was begun? Yet how can directors of a society calculate its growth and progress —the zeal of whose members may die an early death, and the directors not foresee it?

Detestation of some particular persons is the beginning of alienation—which should make members, when they know it, who are desirous of acquiring or retaining associates, careful of their speech and their ways. Will a knowledge even of double entry incline a member to associate with disagreeable persons?

We all know something is wanting. At a late Royal Commission on Labour a high official representative of co-operation was asked whether profits were given to the workers employed by his society. He made answer that "it was not good business to do it" —a reply that a pushing tradesman might make. It excited the amazement of Lord Derby and gentlemen of the Commission, who knew that co-operation was pledged to equity in workshop and store. Co-operation was founded upon that principle—Congress has repeatedly affirmed it. Such an answer would have been impossible, had persons appointed to important office ever been examined in the cardinal principles they openly profess. We all know what a loss it is to the public, that Civil servants undergo no examination in civility: as it is to us when our chief officers are unexamined in co-operation.

A new member will find that a store or workshop is a democracy. An important feature of it is that all members are equally liable to be called upon to serve it, according to their capacity. So desirable was it thought by the early promoters of the Leeds Society that every member should qualify himself for service, that he who refused to take an office to which he was elected, was fined ten shillings and sixpence. This shows that intrinsic co-operative knowledge is not an option, but a necessity. If a member may be elected to office he should understand what is the temper of office? Does he know that masterfulness—the vice of authority—is the death of fraternity? How should he act to maintain that true authority which ensures unity and commands respect?

The holder of office sometimes comes to think that the society is his servant—not he the servant of the society—and regards the members as an inferior class. It was what Shakespeare describes as "the insolence of office," which made the Americans adopt the "spoil system," which enables electors to secure civility by bestowing or withholding office. Yet, repellant as individuals may be, they are to be retained in office if, on the whole, they serve the interests of the society better than anyone else available. Personal disappointment is to be put up with, if the welfare of the society would be endangered by a change. One good of causing the new member to understand the policy of office is that, when his turn of office comes, he may not destroy his usefulness by imperiousness, or vanity of manner.

This is the more important, because permanent officials, familiar with the incidents of administration for long periods, are necessary in every government, and if the heads of departments are not certain of their tenure of office by good service, no man will be vigilant where vigilance brings no security of place. Societies suffer by too frequent changes, and lose the wisdom of long experience in their affairs. Many capricious and disastrous elections are made by reason of members never being informed of these issues, and foolish votes are put down to the caprice of democracy which arise solely from want of knowledge.

Upon the policy of office not even algebra throws any light, nor even freehand drawing affords any guidance. My modest contention is that co-operative education is as distinctive as the moon, and like the moon reveals the aspect of the land, when night renders the path of advancement difficult to discern.

For instance, an elector needs to know that the greatest talker is not always an equally good administrator, and may be a bad man of business. If the good speaker has practical capacity his power of explaining the reasons for any course taken is an advantage to members. It is an old maxim of government that "place reveals the man." A loud declaimer for liberty and better management will sometimes prove an imperious fool in office. It is therefore useful to find out, if you can, the qualities of a man before putting him in power.

Once some negro train attendants found the late Henry George, in plebeian dress, the single passenger in a Pullman car. The ebony group had little expectation of a fee from him, but when he gave them a liberal one—he having overheard they had had a bad time on that train—they were amazed, and the black boss at the head of them exclaimed, "I allis says, and I says it again, you never knows a frog till you sees it jump." So when anyone is to be elected to office, it is prudent to first find out how he jumps. And he will jump well if he has had real co-operative education.

II.—CO-OPERATION SELF-HELPING, SELF-SUBSISTING, AND SELF-CONTAINED.

IN every country there are distinct classes who have no more liking or wish for association with others, than men of Indian castes have. The kind of education wanted is one that conduces to genial comradeship. Cordial association is the strength of co-operation. A member may know all the geological strata of the earth and the latest theory of the origin of mountains, but that will not enable him to tolerate those whom he dislikes. He may know all the stars that astronomy can reveal to him, but there is no obvious incentive to good-will in all the constellations, and good-will is the essence of the co-operative spirit. A member may win a scholarship, and never care for the good of others. A man may have great ability and many acquirements, and yet be a very disagreeable person. Very learned persons are sometimes very great rascals. What was missed in their education or environment, that they did not turn out honest men? A man may be clever, and, as the Duke of Wellington said, be a "clever devil." Co-operative societies have sometimes been robbed by the cleverest men among them. Does biology—most useful science though it be—teach integrity? If not, what kind of instruction may conduce to it? Without association there is neither power nor protection nor emancipation for industry. Association is an art, but it has scant literature and few professors.

The Pioneers of Rochdale were influenced by a simple system of human ethics, which inspired them with that patience and persistence which carried them through the storm and stress of contrary opinion, raging in their time, and enabled them to found that new industrial movement now known as co-operation. From them was derived that principle of toleration and neutrality towards all conviction in religion and politics—without collective partisanship with any, which has made industrial unity possible to this day.

Before and since the time of the Pioneers, co-operation has meant good-will to others—in contradistinction to competition, which means good-will to itself. But good-will to others implies equity—for that would be a shabby sort of good-will which is unjust to anyone. Co-operation signifies, in its very nature, working together—and working together means friendliness; for unfriendly people never work together long. No co-operator is long a member before he meets with persons whom he dislikes, but it is not worth while making much of that. Another person may be disagreeable in your estimation, but unless you happen to be entirely perfect you may seem disagreeable to him. But if there be amity in the heart, diversity does not count. Friendliness is the solvent of repugnance.

Co-operation stands apart, but it is not hostile to others. It climbs the heights to attain a wider view of life and breathe the fresher air of amity—but it has no enmity to those who choose to remain in the valley. It is self-helping, self-sustained, and self-contained. But upon self-help it imposes conditions of regard for the welfare of others. Self-help is predatory, unless good feeling controls it. Shakespeare says, "To thine own self be true." But is it an aggressive "self" or a fraternal "self"? The only self which can be trusted is an educated self, actuated by a sense of truth and a sense of equity. There is no truth without honesty and no equity without justice, which is higher than kindness and nobler than charity. To put into the mind the meaning of these essential terms and promote the practice of their meaning, is co-operative education.

It is not much recognised that co-operation is by its nature self-contained and fraternal. Lately, when a tradesman in Hull added co-operative features to his business, which was a good to his customers and an extension of our principles, it was a matter for

THE SOCIALISTS' INSTITUTE.   THE WEAVERS' ARMS.

WHERE THE FIRST ROCHDALE STORE WAS ORIGINATED.

co-operative gratulation. Yet there were leading co-operators hostile to it, unconscious that our system contains advantages which no private trader can supersede nor imitate, and which place our stores above all rivalry. These independent and self-contained advantages are essential subjects of co-operative teaching.

I am a builder of castles in the air—not only because there is ample space above, but also because there is no landlord who interferes and no ground rent to pay. There are a number of handsome edifices constructed in the sky, and some prove habitable eventually. Now and again discovering eyes are attracted to some goodly aerial design—foundations are dug for it on earth, and the castle in the air becomes a fortress of progress below. Who knows but co-operate education may be one of them?

What are the intrinsic principles of the movement contained within itself?

Co-operation means progress, else why co-operate? A man need not co-operate to stand still, he can do that by himself, but if progress is meant it can only be accomplished by raising the low, and they can only be raised by intelligence. Stupidity limits all progress. Cæsar's army could go no faster on its march, than the asses bearing his commissariat would move. That is true of the march of every movement. The asses always determine the pace. The preacher who has fools for his congregation can only address them in silly similes, and in the end—by the necessity of keeping on their low level—he becomes as foolish as his flock. It is the same with directors of co-operative societies. They can go no faster than the members have sense to permit them, and ignorance is always in a majority. Therefore, if you have no commiseration for inferior natures (which no men choose for themselves) it is good co-operative policy to raise the unfortunate and incapable. The earliest and wisest of co-operative maxims was, that in industry, " Knowledge without Unity is powerless—Unity without Knowledge is helpless." Education, from the first, was a primary part of co-operation—not a caprice, but a policy—not a charity, but a necessity. It was a trade charge.

The will of most men is supine or weak, save when impelled by the passions; but when impelled by right knowledge, it is the eternal element of advancement. It is the will which vivifies life, as electricity vivifies nature; but, like electricity, its energy destroys unless its current be directed by the sense of humanity and equity. It is then the wise inciter, inspirer, impeller, the advancer —the conqueror of apathy and stupidity—the creator of enthusiasm! It is not the "survival" of the fittest, but the creation of the fittest, to which co-operation is committed. This is the co-operative education which is needed.

Good-will is part of the co-operative profession, and can never be divorced from it. It carries the pledge of amity in its name. Without education in the qualities described, co-operation would sink into mere business and be no more an ethical force than mere private trade.

When the Rochdale Society began, a candidate had to be proposed and seconded, and after three months—if nothing became known against him—he was elected a member. The society adopted the precaution from the practice of the Community Society, established by the followers of Robert Owen, of which the chief Rochdale Pioneers were members.

When I was a "social missionary" in those days it was one of my duties to examine all candidates before admission into the societies in my district. I sometimes examined persons of far greater general knowledge than myself. At Bilston, for instance, one candidate was a student of art and a writer of some distinction under the name of " Pencil 'Em," who came to hold a high official position at the South Kensington Museum. But the question of importance to us was, " What did he know of the principles of the new social life which we sought to introduce, and which by his membership he pledged himself to extend by his advocacy and commend by his personal character?" Those were the facts it concerned us to know. In the latest programme for the education of co-operators, does the student find anything having reference to this necessity?

The education fund created by the Pioneers, was to prepare members for *companionship*. They did not require classical, scientific, and historical knowledge in order to sell oatmeal and candles. It was the social education which goes before and after which they had primary need.

Education is not co-operative, because it is given by co-operators to co-operators, unless it is conducive to the formation of the co-operative mind. "A man is ignorant," says Archbishop Tillotson, "however much he may know, if he does not know what it is necessary for him to know."

No one will accuse me of undervaluing general education. The education of the schools is of supreme service in public citizenship, but co-operation is a school of social citizenship, with requirements which erudition does not supply.

III.—IMPORTANCE OF CHARACTER AND METHODS.

DEAN SWIFT was of opinion that it was very difficult to reason a man out of a society, who has been reasoned into it. It is therefore worth while to give new members good reason for steadfastness in the choice they have made. The spirit of association does not come by chance. There must be a reason for it, to render it continuous. That spirit is not put into a man's nature by science classes, as some seem to think. The ear of the musician has to be instructed before it becomes susceptible of the enchantment that lies in sound. The eye of the artist has to be taught before it can see the infinite facts of form, always present and never seen by the untrained vision. In like manner the associative spirit needs to be educated before it can be depended upon. To have unwavering conviction, "a man must," as Coleridge says, "not only know what a thing is, but *why* it is what it is."

The directors in any society, which is to bring about a superior social state, must—Leslie Stephen says—possess the instinct of "public spirit, the hatred of indolence, and be persons of temperance and self-command." What kind of knowledge will best generate these qualities? A knowledge where the red sandstone strata lies, or when the next comet will appear, affords no clue to the conditions of probity, nor inspires any preference for ethical qualities in a leader.

Mr. Stephen contends that "the welfare of every society, the total means of enjoyment at its disposal, depend upon the energy, intelligence, and trustworthiness of its constituent members."* Now "energy and intelligence" may be most pernicious without "trustworthiness," which means the supremacy of moral conviction. Mathematics and technical education, however important in their places, do very little towards the creation of "trustworthiness,"

---

* "Social Rights and Duties," by Leslie Stephen. "Morality of Competition," p. 154, vol. II.

whence it follows that co-operative education includes a class of subjects entirely distinct from instruction in mechanical art. Trustworthiness comes from respecting the pledge of integrity included in the profession of good-will, which is *empty without honesty.*

We have to maintain that quality of store life, in which it shall be a pecuniary advantage and a personal improvement for new members to be associated. If a member finds true men about him he will soon know them. "A rogue does not laugh in the same way that an honest man does; a hypocrite does not shed the same sort of tears as fall from the eyes of a man of good faith. All falsehood is a mask, and however well made the mask may be, with a little attention we may always succeed in distinguishing it from the true face."*

Our societies being constitutionally democratic, makes deference and courtesy towards each other a *necessity* among members, or intercourse would be all rudeness, coarseness, and bear-garden manners. Personal respectfulness is not a common virtue in the House of Commons. Can a workman be expected to acquire, without repeated instruction, the grace and advantage which gave Gladstone his charm and ascendancy in debate? Does anyone read correspondence in our journals, or listen to speeches at quarterly meetings, without feeling that this art is often lacking?

Since members may become leaders in their turn, and are always electors of leaders, the quality of every man and woman in a co-operative society is of paramount importance. The sort of person the elector looks for will depend upon what the elector is himself. Cobden said of Lord Palmerston that he was so impartial that he had no bias—not even towards the truth. But co-operators are the better for that kind of instruction which gives them a bias towards right action.

An intelligence fund is a provision demanded by accepted principle, else members must depend on charity and chance for knowledge, which is contrary to the self-helping independence co-operation is intended to create.

A store is commonly conceived to be a society of shop-keepers, chiefly concerned for a dividend, devoid of a social idea, without which higher life is unknown, unthought of, and unattainable. Still, we retain something of the Pioneer passion for loftier things, and have made the store system into a cause. In most stores now there is a soul higher than dividends, legitimate and important as dividends are. Not even the duty of buying at the store is personally impressed on new members. The Leeds Society has a prudent rule (which many societies lack) that a member must purchase to the amount of £8 a year, or his membership ceases; otherwise the interest on his shares, and the subscription paid to the Union for the protection of his interests (so long as his name stands in the books) falls upon other members. Loans are made to societies, and interest has to be paid upon them. Unless adequate purchases are made, these expenses cannot be met. In many societies not half are purchasing members. Each member should

---

* Dumas, "Three Musketeers," chap. 25.

understand from the first, that the business interest of the society can only be maintained by due purchases. Some interrogating person should stand, as it were, at the gate of the society. If the new adherent joins it from curiosity, that sentiment should be satisfied; if for information, it should be given; if for dividend, it should be explained how it can be earned; if to aid in establishing concord between labour and wealth, that object should be commended and confirmed. South tells us that "a good inclination is the first crude draught of virtue." The act of joining us is the first overture of an adherent, who, if neglected, is commonly lost. To retain him, he must be informed. Certainly not five hundred in fifty thousand who join our societies, are ever personally spoken to upon the duties of membership.

It is then each should be asked to take in the *Co-operative News* as a thing expected of him. Were he joining a joint-stock society, which made him 5 per cent. on his investment—he would have to buy his shares at a premium. In a co-operative society he has no premium to pay though it makes him 10 per cent. on his purchases. In an ordinary financial society a member readily takes in the *Joint-Stock Circular* or the *Financial News*, or any organ which informs him of the prosperity of his investment. As a co-operative society makes profit for him without cost to himself he ought to be told that the *Co-operative News* would be sent to him with his weekly purchases. In many of our societies not more than one in a hundred of the members take in the official organ of co-operation. If all new members were required to take the paper, the circulation of the representative journal would augment beyond all experience. By calculations Mr. Gray has made for me, it appears that during the ten years between 1886 and 1897 the average of new members joining the societies amounted to 58,000 annually. If only half of them took in the paper its circulation would increase nearly 30,000 a year, and they would—if solicited to do so on joining. That may be done at the beginning which can never be done afterwards. The new member is admitted into a movement now no longer obscure or precarious—but famous and prosperous.

We have now probably a hundred editors of store journals, and editorial policy is therefore a matter of moment. To answer correspondents in the second person is an offence to a public reader, who has a private conversation forced upon him. No letter should be inserted unless the editor is prepared to insert an answer of the same quality. No dishonouring imputation should ever appear, as incurable hostilities arise thereby. No person giving his name on a personal question, should ever be allowed to be answered by one who withholds his, as it opens the door to spite and cowardice, in which amateur co-operators sometimes indulge. Journalism will increase as stores and workshops extend, and some knowledge of its laws is part of co-operative education.

Neutrality as to politics and religion is a necessity in a union of members of all parties. In co-operation, as in a king's speech, nothing can be proposed which may not be discussed, since projects undiscussed are never understood. The opinion of a person who knows only one side of a subject can never be trusted. But on the absorbing subjects of party policy and religious belief, discussion would be an unending and ever-dividing digression from social work, which needs all the strength of unity. Members require education in neutrality, which is only possible to the instructed and fair. Journals pledged to neutrality will admit articles on religion which from the other side would never be admitted. Intense bits of theology can be dropped into a story, or into an argument, or appear in a quotation. My first public letter to the Chamber Brothers, long years ago, was on this practice, who in their works violated the neutrality they professed. I found it was conventional and not intellectual neutrality they meant to observe. Fairness to the majority is always sure, but fairness to the minority is a very rare virtue, and education in it is a source of strength and unity in co-operative literature; for neutrality is not a gift, it means trained capacity in the art of impartiality.

The life, the interests, and the instruction of our committees and board meetings would be greater were the motions made briefly reported, and brief abstracts of the arguments used. Foolishness would decrease, which now often prevails, and good sense find honour and imitation. Whereas now the poorest, driest, bare-bone reports kill all interest in such meetings. Every Anglo-Indian reformer tells us that it is by omissions in reports that misrule is kept up. Without open information all along the line there can be no live society. We see to-day what has come to the Spanish people by being fed on a diet of lies. A diet of omissions is also dangerous to the public health. The faculty of publicity is only developed by instruction and cultivation. Our societies would have twice the local influence they have, were there always about someone who knows when to take occasions by the hand which would interest those outside.

It is surely part of co-operative education to instruct a member in the duties he will be called upon to discharge, and the reasons which should influence him. For instance, money has to be voted at our meetings. To whom?—for what?—and why? are worthy of consideration.

Lately the Army and Navy Supply Association had a surplus, which the directors, being just-minded, did not think it right to appropriate to their own use, but gave it away to *remote charities*. All the while nothing was given to their own employés, whose industry and faithfulness had helped to make the surplus. Is any co-operative society justified in voting money *outside* itself, where its own servants received no share of its gains? Unless participation exists, it is the money of workers which is given away.

Rich men build churches, while those who made their wealth come to premature graves because of insufficient means of life. Well intended are the gifts to the church or the park, to hospital or library. But were all the workmen properly requited, they would give these things to themselves—and old age pensions too. As charity now stands, the real donors are mainly the workmen, who made the riches of the givers.

IV.—PRINCIPLE ENSURES PROGRESS AND PRECLUDES DESPAIR.

E have scientific lectures now. Why does no one explain to members how to buy at the stores, and the signs whereby the purchaser shall know what he is buying? Were there no ignorant buying there would be no fraudulent selling anywhere. Thousands of our store members are at times discontented with what is served to them, through not knowing what genuineness is when they get it. That co-operative education is not very prevalent was shown lately by Mr. William Cussons, of Hull. No tradesman has excelled him in adapting the methods of co-operation in his business. Yet he recently told us that the division of profit in a store was an advertisement device, and did not know it was an essential principle. A great society in an eastern county, which honourably gave participation in its profits to its servants, afterwards abandoned it. The editor of its local "Record" cited me as "opposed to the bonus principle," whereas I had merely objected to participation being called by the name of "bonus," which means a charity, and not a right. Did he not know the distinction? Though thrice requested, he never published my letter pointing out the error, and the members have been left to this day under the belief that the directors have my authority for their abandonment of an essential store principle. Had the members ever had real co-operative education, they would have known the principle themselves. Yet we have held a Congress in that town.

That only is complete co-operation where the principle of division of profits in the store is extended to all in its service, and where workers share in profits, capital, and control—that is the higher form of co-operation, because it calls forth higher powers, and conduces to the development of higher character, and because it gives to the worker—who better deserves it—the same advantage it gives to the consumer.

Competition denies that labour has a right to anything beyond its wages, but co-operation, which concedes the right of profits to the purchaser, who gives nothing save his custom towards producing them, cannot rightly withhold participation from the worker, who gives his labour to creating them. Anyhow, the co-operator is bound to have an opinion on this subject, and should have the information given him upon which to form it.

The co-operative principle of equity is as old as Spinoza, who said, "Desire nothing for yourself which you do not desire for others." Does not this sentiment require special teaching? Will new members ever practice it who are never made aware of its nobleness? Co-operation, as I have said, implies a new sense—that of not taking from the worker his share of the profit of his industry, because it can be done with impunity, because custom sanctions it, and because the worker is unable to resist it.

It is easy to withhold from servants or workpeople any share of the profit of their labour. Many are too ignorant to know that industry has rights as well as property. Many are too abject to stand up for their right if they knew it—the majority are too dependent to make a claim—they would lose their situation if they did. If anyone takes the earnings of the rich it is called thieving, and properly so, but to take the property of others who are unable to resist it, passes under the name of "good business." No one proposes to take the profit from the store members, because they would soon go elsewhere; but the profit can be taken from the workshop, because workmen cannot readily find other situations.

There is something to be said upon the other side. Well-intending persons defend the withholding of profit from workers, but they defend it by capitalistic, not co-operative arguments. They constitute a company for running "Co-operative Principle Limited." Its doctrine is "All for the consumer," which, if carried out, would arrest all propagandism—put an end to all lectures, stop all educational funds and all subscriptions to the Union, since the expense of these things diminishes the dividends of the consumers, who have a right to the profits of trade, but not to the profit of labour. The doctrine of all for the consumer is, in the famous words of Henry Clay, "blowing out the moral lights around us." The late Judge Hughes, to whom the doctrine was abhorrent, called it a "Guts Gospel." There are two sides to this question, as to most others. All I contend for is that a member should be well informed upon both.

Anyone who has taken sides in any battle of progress, knows that the great essentials of a party that wants to win, are principles. These alone are the permanent source of enthusiasm. Without principles a party dies.

In a great northern society, where a proposal was made to join the Wholesale, an official speaker said to the members: "It was not to their interest, and therefore, was not their duty, to do it."* Many, besides this chairman, consider that interest is the measure of duty, and say so without being met with quick dissent. This shows that education in principle has not proceeded far.

Co-operative trade stands upon honesty, and when honest business does not pay it is no business for honest men. He who cheats, steals, and is a thief. As respects truth the law is absolute. A man may hold his peace, but if he speaks he must not lie. However little profit a society makes, it must be honest. What principle is in public affairs, honesty is in business. Without honesty, politics or trade sinks into a disreputable calling. Higher co-operation is where principle is adhered to, and where adherence is a policy.

I have witnessed a council of leaders in our movement give an important contract outside, when it could be well executed within, they deciding in favour of the cheapest tender. Yet excellence, and not cheapness, should rule preferences. The choice of mere cheapness is the deterioration of stores.

Socialism and co-operation are alien in principle. It is not necessary here to decide between them, only to state the distinction between them. Education is not propagandism, but information.

---

* Leeds Jubilee History. Agesilaus, King of Sparta, excited abhorrence in Athens by saying, "What was good for Sparta, was right."

Without that, a man may have the confusion of mind of Gohre the German, who is for combining God's help, brotherly help, self-help, and State-aid.

It is not unusual to see someone interrupt a speaker on a point of order or etiquette, which has never been defined. A Standing Orders Committee may consist of persons who never met before, and whose predecessors left no record of their principles of procedure. But these and many other questions which will occur to the informed reader, I do not stay to describe, lest I prolong this address unduly.

Impatience is the mother of co-operative disaster in communities, as well as in stores and workshops. In the United States impetuosity often puts back a new cause. Even in Italy social enthusiasm has its reactions. Rabbeno, in his latter days, confessed to disappointed expectation. An ardent but uninstructed reformer rises in the morn, looks out, sees the industrial world going wrong. He gives it a stout push in what he surmises is the right direction. After a while he looks out again, and finds it has got back into its old track. He is discouraged, and concludes it is no use pushing any more, whereas perverse things want repeated pushing before they go as they ought. It was an impetuous horticulturist who, having planted a shrub over night, took it up next morning to see whether it had taken root. The shrub of co-operation often requires an unconscionable time to take root. A new principle is dilatory in growing. The best of seeds will not quicken anywhere. The fault is less in the seed than in the conditions of its culture. A new system, like a new character, cannot be formed right off. Character, like an electric light, does not burn without a continuous current, and care has to be taken that the current be not diverted elsewhere.

Twelve years ago there was a co-operative society in " Oshkosh, Wis.," which I suppose means Wisconsin. It had headquarters, its president, secretary, twelve directors, an Oshkosh organ, and 142 members. Who hears of the society of Oshkosh now? How many societies have gone up like the rocket and come down like the stick, to whom co-operative education would have given longer luminousness?

The Scotch, with sagacious conscientiousness, when they give change lay it out before you in crowns, florins, or shillings, so that you can see what you are receiving, and that the amount is exact. The English give you change in a lump, and unless you count it before them or when you get home, you never know what you have received. The Scotch say the " English give change as a job lot." Most co-operative societies take their members as a "job lot," providing, neither before joining nor after, any systematic instruction in co-operative ideas. When they go wrong on some question of duty and progress, they are reproached for their "lack of principle," forgetful that they never had it. Fortunately, a considerable number of our members have educated themselves by lectures and books, in the essentials of the co-operative system. None know better than they, that upon job lot members no committee can count.

It is Utopian to think that some instruction in the essentials of co-operative requirements would prevent our societies being over-run by haphazard, miscellaneous, unsorted, uninstructed members of the job lot kind?

Few things are more pathetic than to see advocates who have made great sacrifices for the cause, become despondent because those whom they have sought to serve seem to care nothing for the advantages offered to them. As I have said elsewhere, when was it otherwise? The Apostles were badly treated for their offer of a new gospel. Nobody wanted Magna Charta except a few barons. A few farmers and lawyers of public spirit and self-respect were the chief persons who carried American Independence. It required all the eloquence of Paine to inspire the middle class with a desire for it. Only a few slaves, scattered over distant plantations, had spirit enough to wish to be free. The majority preferred slavery, so long as they had plenty of food and were not much whipped. The preference our trade unions manifest for hired labour over the co-operative share of profits, shows the prevalence of the slave spirit. What is a hired labourer

> But a slave without his chains?
> The badge is cancelled, but the slave remains.*

It seems to me incredible that anyone who believes himself to be on the right road should turn back because those do not accompany him whom he expected. Those go ever onward who once have

> Looked with steady gaze
> On the sunlight lying beyond the haze.

Those who see that competition and co-operation are not two methods of business, but imply different systems of society, will never know supineness or despair.

"Do not be afraid of benefiting men," says Guicciardini, "simply because you see ingratitude so common; for besides that a temper of kindness in itself, and without any other object, is a generous quality, and in a way divine, you now and again find somebody exhibiting such gratitude as richly to make up for all the ingratitude of all the rest!" Drawing back from conferring advantages to those not likely to appreciate them, has robbed the grateful portion of mankind of a million benefits.

The Italian has two gifts—one in his throat, where song is born, and the other in his hand, which excels in art.

The German has persistence in his will, which carries him far.

The Dutchman has it in his nature, and is always to be counted upon.

The Frenchman's gift is in his eye, who sees quicker and more accurately than a man of any other race.

Let us hope that the gift of the English shall be known by skill in social device, especially that of progress by reason and self-help—that we shall endow English industry with a charter of participation which creates equality without spoliation. Browning says, "God fashioned us to help each other, lending out our minds." And real co-operative education will give us minds worth lending out.

---

* Last poem of Ernest Jones.

JUDGE HUGHES.

V.—THE BELIEF OF THE EARLY PIONEERS.

OW co-operation is self-acting, it may interest curious readers to learn what was the intellectual belief of the early Pioneers and of the men of their time in every part of the country, whose educated energy created the stores, set the movement going, and stood by it amid the storm of intimidating opinion which assailed it. The churches distrusted and decried every project of social reform which they did not control. To adopt any form of Christianity (could it be done 'at will) was to limit co-operation to a sect. No church would act with another—nor act with any party—unless its tenets were to prevail. Besides, it was thought that ideas of improvement made the poor discontented with that " condition of life to which it had pleased Providence to call them." Trust in self-help was considered of the nature of sin, since its tendency was to prevent men from looking above for aid. The effect of environment on character was not only disbelieved ; it was denounced. Very few thought well of Shelley after he had written,

Men are the sport of circumstance, when
Circumstance seems the sport of men.

Now, a new environment for industry was the sole hope and aim of co-operation. This was a new cause of ire. It was in vain to plead that the end sought was moral. Morality was no plea in mitigation of orthodox judgment. It was a new offence. Nobody believed in the independence of morality. It was, therefore, necessary to create a new class of persons who would work with anybody for a moral end, without attempting to impose all their individual convictions upon others. There was no hope of establishing any new movement worth living in, except among men who would stand up for right conduct, or reasoned truth, for its own sake—a perilous thing to do, as Sir Charles Lyell knew, who had to withhold for twenty years, his proof of the antiquity of the world.

Had not co-operators purchased their own library books, they would not have been allowed to read what they pleased. Had they not built halls for themselves, their quarterly meetings would often have had to be held in field or street ; and lectures would, in most places, have been impossible. Had not the Pioneers thought for themselves, there had been no Rochdale Store. They knew, with Shakespeare, that " words without thoughts never to heaven go." They had thoughts of self-help, and trusted them. That was their creed. It seems like a new world now. Ministers and prelates preach to us like gentlemen, neither concealing nor obtruding their opinions. Everyone is free to believe what he can, and say the thing he will, in relevance, not violating the equal right of others.

Save one (Dr. Frederick Hollick) I alone remain to tell what the opinions of the Pioneers were. In 1840 I (with Lloyd Jones, Dr. John Watts, and others) was one of the official teachers of co-operation. Our chief object was the formation of associative character. To this end, like the Prophet Esdras, we concerned ourselves with " what passed by us in daily life." What happens there? A man finds himself confronted by persons of infinite diversity of character, tendency, and passion—diversity ever perplexing, tendency ever drifting in a predetermined direction. Whence, then, have come these mysterious qualities? No one had any choice when, or where, or of whom, he would be born. Existence is thrust upon men by a power unseen and unknown. The lot of the majority of mankind is incapacity, ignorance, disease, and poverty, which means subjugation and toil. What is the good, or the sense, or the humanity, of hating the unfortunate any more than in hating a clock which is false to time, owing to defective machinery? Those who have received an inferior nature and an unhappy destiny have no demerit therein, since their condition is their misfortune, and not their fault. Those who are fortunate in inheriting health and opulence have no merit on that account, since it was neither their selection nor their desert. The fortunate mostly show contempt of those inferior to themselves; whereas their only feeling—if they had instructed feeling—would be pity for all below them, and it would be, were it not for the belief that the perversities of men proceed from their wilfulness. These perversities, which destroy all respect for them in so many minds—how do they arise, save in the nature which they inherit, and in the circumstances which debase them, neither of which did they make? " Environment," says Goethe, " is a sculptor which shapes all humanity." Even the most intractable of all the qualities of the human mind— the religious sentiment—bends before environment, and is subdued by it, and takes the form of the Chinese, the Buddhist, the Jewish, or Moslem faith. If it be not so, why do we send missionaries abroad to create the environment of another faith? Unless circumstances tell on character, why are we told that " evil communications corrupt good manners"?

All education is comprised in two words—*train* and *restrain*. From the first, co-operation has had in view to create that condition of life in which it shall be impossible for men to be depraved or poor.

In a conversation with John Arthur Roebuck on this subject, he said to me: " I well remember going one morning down my garden in Bath, to our nurse's house, and seeing her child and my child lying in cots side by side. In vigour and appearance the nurse's child had more promise than mine, then a little wizened * thing. Yet the nurse's daughter will become a servant girl, and mine will be a lady. Why will that be? The different circumstances in which they will be reared will make the difference. Who can explain why this should be? Who can deny that it is so?" I have never forgotten these impressive words. Why, then, should animosity arise in the heart at beholding the inevitableness of destiny and diversity?

Personal dislike, so fatal to association, comes from the belief that diversity is born of perversity. It is in vain any are told " to love their enemies." None will do it; none can do it; none ought to do it who believe that the enmity which pursues them proceeds

---

* The graphic word has never left my memory.

from an evil heart, which he who has it could change, or get changed, if he would, but will not. If that be true, anger, blame, dislike, and resentment are justifiable. If, in matters of religions—which move men beyond all others—a man can believe as he pleases, and will not believe as I please, his refusal puts distrust and dislike between us.† If he makes himself repugnant by his own wilfulness, how can there be confidence in association with him? Therefore, the co-operators seek for human reasons of reconcilement, which can be seen, known, and understood by men of all persuasions alike; so that unity shall be based on a foundation that cannot be moved.

In the days when I first joined in teaching this doctrine of tolerance, I was asked: "Suppose anyone is intentionally insulted, wronged, or defamed with 'malice aforethought,' as lawyers put it, can the insulted like the insultor?" I answered "No, he will not be likely to like him, and will avoid him as far as possible. Repugnance to him will be felt, because he is believed to be consciously base." But how came he to be base by nature, when he might have been endowed with nobleness and fairness? Is it not his misfortune that he inflicts on himself alienation, distrust, and avoidance? Is it necessary that we increase further the injuries of his malevolent destiny? Is there no reason, if opportunity offers, to compensate somewhat for the calamity of his disposition? If a man does not make his own defects, he does not, therefore, escape the consequences of them. If he violates the laws he will be repressed. The snake did not give himself his venom; but if he attempts to bite us we kill him, despite his beauty and sinuous grace of motion. If a man be mad, hatred dies when we understand his misfortune.

Yet man being dominated by circumstance does not close the gates of progress. On the contrary, it leaves them wide open. His will is susceptible of direction, and that is the eternal element of improvement. Impressive evidence stimulates and changes him. Will is but the susceptibility of the understanding determined to action by vivid impressions of evidence and reason. This is the hope of the Apostles and the Reformers. The right environment, mental and material, is the moving force of all advancement. Swift's "Tale of a Tub" created a new character in Cobbett. Seeing the ruins of the Colosseum determined Gibbons to write the "Decline and Fall of the Roman Empire." Even those who say the will is free, act in education as though it was influenced by reason, else the teacher or preacher would never reason with anyone, and the philosopher would be dumb.

If man has not a *caused* will, but has independent spontaneous power of acting without reasons; if he can act on facts without knowing them, there is no need for the preacher, the teacher, or the lecturer. They are foolish and impertinent praters, who take trouble which must be futile. All they need do is to tell a man to act as they wish, and then go home; and even telling would be

† This is the only sense in which Robert Owen ever said the religions of the world were wrong. Bentham, who had knowledge of these questions, sent word to Francis Place, "Every man is master of his own actions, but no man of his own opinions."

needless unless the telling be a circumstance. An uncaused will is the doctrine of fools, and, if consistently acted upon, would fill the world with idiots.

Against incapacity and hostility, anger is no remedy. Anger is but ignorance taken by surprise. Resentment has no light in it and breeds retaliation. Unless some higher view stills anger and resentment, permanent fraternity is hopeless. The meanest and the noblest teachers of religion alike praise the holiness of anger and the justice of resentment. Where that doctrine is in action, fraternity is dead. Anger and resentment—the natural forces of the savage—have had a long reign, through the fear that sympathy was connivance. But pity does not mean impunity to wrong. A man may hate wrong, and have sorrow for the wrongdoer. There is a discriminating compassion which keeps no terms with crime.

The want of an angerless tolerance and commiseration for inferior natures, has been the ruin of communities of social life again and again. More governments are wrecked and more good measures defeated in Church and State, as well as in co-operative societies, by personal animosities than by difference of principles.

Pascal, in a memorable passage, explains : " What an enigma is man ! What a strange, chaotic, and contradictory being ! Judge of all things, feeble earthworm, depository of the truth, mass of uncertainty, glory of the universe, incomprehensible monster !" But few seem to see that every man has *all* these qualities of his race within him, and that it is the aim and inspiration of education to diminish the baser elements and strengthen the nobler. Compassion founded on discernment of heredity and environment goes not back. Seeing how differences have their origin in nature and not in the will, a noble, changeless tolerance enters the mind—not the tolerance based on charity, which may be withdrawn, but a tolerance based on justice, which is the right of humanity. Intelligent compassion has the remediable instinct, and strives to create those conditions which only commiseration conceives. Sympathy is the key to attention. All men are won by unreproaching help. Varying the words of the poet, we may say :—

> Take compassion in thy hand,
> No human anger can withstand
> One touch of that magic wand.

Millions of men in every clime are bound to the past by an unseen chain, from which no man can free himself. Men not only leave the world, they come into it, " with imperfections on their head." Not one among them, had the choice been given him, but would have chosen strength and capacity, comeliness and prosperity, courage and self-direction, and the eternal charm of conscious power, which is a perpetual letter of recommendation to all men. Can anyone think of the great mass of mankind doomed, with so many disadvantages, to bear the burden of the world, and not exclaim with Saadi : " *O God have mercy on the bad. Thou has done everything for the good in making them good.*"

*   *   *

To these principles the public owed the generosity of Robert Owen, who gave his great wealth for the benefit of those who assailed him by every form of speech and prayer. To these principles, the co-operative cause owed the angerless voice of William Pare (who was deprived of his Registrarship because he held them)— the greatest of those who gave the movement its self-contained independence. To the same principles we owed the cheeriness and undespairingness of James Smithies, and the courage and propagandist fervour of William Cooper, who thought it the holiest duty to raise inferior natures by kindness and service. A Sunday School teacher myself, and devoutly Christian for many years, no faith, nor prayer, nor precept ever stilled anger or hatred or despair in my heart, as when compassion for the unchosen destiny of mankind entered it. I do not say these views are true. It would be wrong to do that, where my business is simply to describe them. Right or wrong, they had the merits of teaching early co-operators to regard without dislike, distrust, or contempt, the religious views of any who brought the separate sanctions of his conscience to the duty of advancing a just cause.

The Abbé Lamennais, writing of a famous book, depicting the "Passive" Christian, said, "The active Christian who is ceaselessly fighting the enemies of humanity without omitting *to pardon and love them*, of this type of Christian, I find no trace whatever."

The type did not exist in the Pioneer days, and in our wilful and imperfect way we sought to create it in co-operative sociology. Many of us indeed asserted that co-operation was true Christianity, but nobody believed it any more than they believed Lamennais. Such is the history of the principles of early co-operative education.

G. J. HOLYOAKE.

❧ PUBLICATIONS. ❧

PRICE

LABOUR CO-PARTNERSHIP (Monthly)	1d.
Model Rules specially prepared for Co-partnership Productive Societies	1½d.
Annual Report, 8th, 9th, 10th, 11th, 12th, or 13th .. .. 2d. *each*	
Lecture List	*Free*
Co-operative Workshops in Great Britain. 1898. By THOMAS BLANDFORD	3d.
How Co-operative Production may be successfully applied to the Building Trade	1d.
Evidence given by the Labour Association before the Royal Commission on Labour, with introduction	2d.
A New Industrial World. By HODGSON PRATT	1d.
The Co-partnership of Labour (Reprint of Article in *Economic Review*). By HENRY VIVIAN and ANEURIN WILLIAMS	2d.
True Position of Employees in the Co-operative Movement. By H. VIVIAN	1d.
Some Aspects of the Co-operative Movement. By H. VIVIAN ..	1d.
What Co-operative Production is Doing. By H. VIVIAN ..	1d.
Objects and Methods of the Co-operative Movement	1d.
Co-operation as a Democratic Force. By Rev. RAMSDEN BALMFORTH ..	1d.
Co-operative Production Viewed in the Light of some First Principles. By ROBERT HALSTEAD	1d.
How to Start a Co-operative Workshop .. .. 1/6 per 100	
"Members One of Another." By ARCHDEACON WILSON	1d.
The Principles, Objects, and Methods of the Labour Association. By E. V. NEALE. Including short Sketch of Mr. NEALE's Life, with Portrait	2d.
Sixty Years of Co-operation. By SYBELLA GURNEY	1d.
Government by the Fit. By A. WILLIAMS	1d.
Partnership of Capital and Labour as a Solution of the Conflict Between Them. By HENRY VIVIAN	1d.
The Relation of the Church to Co-operation. By EARL GREY ..	1d.
The Essentials of Co-operative Education. By G. J. HOLYOAKE ..	2d.
The Store, the Workshop, and the Trade Union. By F. MADDISON, M.P.	1d.
Labour Co-partnership. By JAMES BONAR, L.L.D.	1d.
Thirty Years' Experience of Industrial Conciliation and Arbitration. By SIR DAVID DALE	1d.
Most of the foregoing Pamphlets, well bound	1/6

LEAFLETS.

What is Co-partnership, and what it can do for the Worker?
Present Position of Co-operative Production.
Trade Unionism and Co-operative Production.
Duties of Workers in Co-partnership Societies.
Appeal to Co-operative Workers.
What the Labour Association does for Co-operation.

Special Terms for Quantities of the above.

The following may be obtained from the Association:—

Labour Co-partnership. By HENRY DEMAREST LLOYD. 350 pages, illustrated. 5/-, by post 5/4.
The History of the Rochdale Pioneers. By G. J. HOLYOAKE. New Edition. Revised and brought up to date. Cloth, 2/-; or 2/3 by post.
Self-Help a Hundred Years Ago. By G. J. HOLYOAKE. Cloth, 2/-; or 2/3 by post.
The Co-operative Movement To-day. By G. J. HOLYOAKE. Cloth, 2/-; or 2/3 by post.
Sixty Years of an Agitator's Life. By G. J. HOLYOAKE. Two vols., cloth, 5/2; or 5/9 by post.
Public Speaking and Debate. By G. J. HOLYOAKE. Price 2/8; or 3/- post free.
History of the Leeds Co-operative Society. 1/6; or 1/10 by post.
A People's Bank Manual. By HENRY W. WOLFF. 6d.; by post, 7d.
Co-operative Credit Banks. By HENRY W. WOLFF. 6d.; by post, 7d.
Frederick Denison Maurice and Christian Socialism. By Rev. E. B. HUGH JONES. One Penny.

If you are interested, write to the Secretary—

15, SOUTHAMPTON ROW, HOLBORN, LONDON, W.C.

☞ **READ**

"THE PRINCIPLES, OBJECTS, AND METHODS
OF THE LABOUR ASSOCIATION,"

BY ITS FIRST PRESIDENT,

MR. E. VANSITTART NEALE,

With which is included a Portrait of Mr. NEALE, and an Account
of his labours on behalf of Co-operative Production.

SEND FOR

The Labour Association's Pamphlet on

"HOW TO START A CO-OPERATIVE
WORKSHOP."

"LABOUR CO-PARTNERSHIP,"

MONTHLY, ONE PENNY.

Post Free, 1/6 a Year, of the Publishers, 15, Southampton Row
Holborn, London, W.C.

Why Social Reformers should Read it.

BECAUSE it is the only organ devoted to the principle; and that
principle offers a tried solution of the Labour Problem.

BECAUSE it deals not with the theory only, but gives reliable
information on the position and progress of nearly 200 Co-
operative Productive Societies, employing some thousands of
workers, and doing a trade of £2,700,000 per annum, where
the principle is being successfully applied.

BECAUSE it contains information on the progress of the principle
abroad, interesting Historical Sketches of Co-operative Productive Societies, Articles by Leading Co-operators, Reviews
of Books on Social and Labour Questions, and other information valuable to all interested in their Social Progress.

Nottingham Co-operative Printing Society, Ltd., 61, Hounds Gate.

CPSIA information can be obtained at www.ICGtesting.com
Printed in the USA
LVOW131856150911

246288LV00002BA/51/P